Before you begin ...

Dear Reader,

Before you begin this Chronicle, you should know that Biff, Chip, Kipper and friends have become Time Runners. They are based in the Time Vault, a place that exists outside time. Their mission is to travel back in time to defeat the Virans.

Virans are dark energy in human form. Their aim is to destroy history and so bring chaos to the future.

The Time Runners have to be brave and self-reliant. They have a Zaptrap, which is a device to capture the Virans. They also have a Link, which is a bit like a mobile phone disguised as a yo-yo. The Link lets them communicate with the Time Vault. Apart from that, when on a mission, they are very much on their own!

Theodore Mortlock

Time Guardian

Baghdad, 8th Century AD

The city of Baghdad was founded in 762 AD. A giant library was built there, called the House of Wisdom. Its aim was to collect and translate books from all over the world. The hope was that Baghdad would become a leading centre of learning and discovery.

Chapter 1

I t was late. Neena was worn out. She had been helping Tyler sort out the books in the Time Vault library. "So many of them!" she sighed as she climbed up a ladder with a handful of books. "Whoops!" Two of the books slipped and fell to the floor. "Sorry!"

Tyler leaned out of his techno-chair to pick up the books Neena had dropped. Most books in the library were about history. He had spent days sorting them out. Then he had numbered them and arranged them so that he knew where each one was.

"There's nothing we can't find out about the history of the world," he said, proudly.

Neena grinned. "But not from the dusty books on this old pile," she said. "They are all in strange languages."

Tyler smiled. "A lot of these books are ancient – hundreds of years old." He picked up a battered folder of faded papers covered in strange writing and symbols that looked a bit like numbers.

"I think this one is written in Sanskrit – it must be from Ancient India," he said. Then his stomach turned over. "Neena! Look!"

"Don't tell me you can read Sanskrit," Neena laughed.

"No, not that," said Tyler. "Something just happened to the writing itself."

Within a moment it happened again. Before their eyes the numbers faded to nothing and then returned to normal.

Neena shuddered. "What does it mean?"

Tyler frowned. "It's as if it's about to disappear. About to be wiped out by ..."

"By Virans?" interrupted Neena.

"These numbers must be important," said Tyler. "What if the numbers were to do with a discovery in science or maths sometime in the past? A Viran might be trying to stop the discovery. That could be why the numbers are fading here. They are in danger of disappearing – wiped from history!"

Neena ran through the library. "Come on, Tyler, let's check the TimeWeb."

Chapter 2

"It's a mystery!" muttered Tyler, tapping the keys of the Matrix. "There's no sign of trouble."

"Are you sure those papers were from India?" said Neena. "Why not do a general search? If we find nothing, we'll call Mortlock."

Tyler tapped the search key. The TimeWeb slowly turned in front of them.

They didn't have to wait long. Low down on the web was a small bruise of darkness. "There!" shouted Tyler. He flicked on the globe. "The 8th Century AD. The newly-built city of Baghdad. Not India after all!"

Neena grabbed her Link and Zaptrap. "Send me out! Now!" she demanded. "I'll check it out. If I need help, you can wake the others."

Chapter 3

From the shadows of an alley, a flock of white doves took flight. As the doves soared into the evening sky, Baghdad stretched out beneath them. The dusty pattern of narrow streets, canals, and market squares was lit by thousands of tiny lanterns. Below the doves, the river Tigris flowed lazily past.

At the river's edge, a dark figure pulled aside a grating and stepped into the underground water channel that ran beneath the city.

The doves flew on over a large circular palace. Then they flew back to the alley where they had taken off.

If anyone had watched where the doves landed, they would have seen Neena step out of the shadows, pull a shawl around her face and join the crowded street.

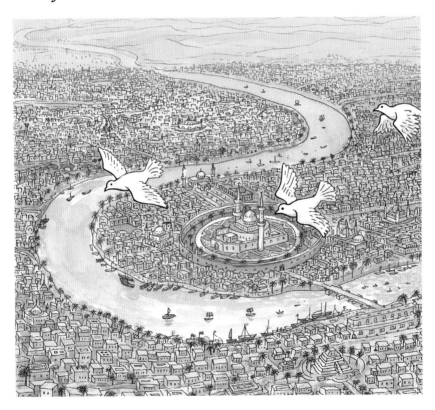

Neena looked around excitedly. There were people everywhere. They crowded around stalls packed with delicious smelling foods and spices, colourful silks and jewellery. There were even stalls selling the latest invention from China – paper!

"Tyler?" Neena whispered into her Link. "Where do I start? The Virans could be anywhere. I haven't got a chance."

From the Link, Tyler's voice sounded thin and distant. "We know it has something to do with that old paper we found in the library," he said. "That's our only clue."

"Maybe there's a library or something here?" wondered Neena.

But before Tyler had time to reply, Neena had to snap the Link shut. Someone was shouting at her. "Hey! Make way! Books for the House of Wisdom!"

Everyone cleared the middle of the street as a line of camels walked through, led by a small girl. The animals swayed under the weight of the heavy wooden chests they were carrying.

Some of the chests were open. They were full of books and scrolls. "Hmm," thought Neena. "Whatever the House of Wisdom is, it seems like a good place to start."

Chapter 4

There was no mistaking the House of Wisdom. It was the magnificent circular palace at the far end of the city. Neena followed the camels and watched as they were unloaded. As they rested, the camels drank deeply from a water channel that came from beneath the palace wall.

DOWNLOAD FROM TYLER

The House of Wisdom – huge library run by world's leading scholars. Get this! They translate written stuff from all round the known world!

The sound of raised voices made Neena look up. The camel girl was arguing with a guard at the gates. Neena crouched behind one of the wooden chests to hear what they were saying.

"The House of Wisdom is closed," snapped the guard. "In the last two nights precious papers on mathematics have been stolen from the library. Everywhere is under guard."

"But we need to be paid," protested the girl. "We have brought many books for the library, all the way from Greece."

"I don't care how far you've travelled," sneered the guard. "Come back tomorrow."

Tyler listened to Neena over the Link. "Do you think the old paper we saw was one of the things stolen?" she whispered.

"No," replied Tyler. "It's still OK. I can

still see the writing, so it can't have been destroyed. Maybe the Virans haven't found it yet. But you can be sure they'll try again."

"But if everywhere is under guard," asked Neena, "how did the Virans get in?"

"Maybe it's an inside job," replied Tyler.

"But how can I get inside to find out?" said Neena. "The gates are guarded."

At that moment, a man in long robes walked angrily towards the guard. He was one of the library scholars. Something about him made Neena feel uneasy.

The scholar pointed at the camel driver. "Wait! We will take the books now. But you must wait outside!"

Neena saw her chance. She climbed inside a half-empty chest and closed the lid.

Chapter 5

It was cramped and stuffy inside the chest, but at last it was dropped heavily on the ground. "At least I am inside the library walls," Neena thought.

She lifted the lid and peeked out. She was in a large courtyard surrounded by many arches, each lit with a brass lantern.

Within every arch, people were busy writing or reading, talking or teaching.

To her horror, she caught sight of the
scholar. He was opening each chest in turn
and examining the contents. The scholar
moved closer, muttering to himself. Neena
carefully closed her lid.

She sat in the cramped darkness. Her hand
found her Zaptrap. She held her breath and
waited. At last, she heard the scholar's hands
touch the lid of the chest she was hiding in.

"This is it," she thought.

The lid opened slightly. The scholar's fingers curled inside. Neena was terrified, but strangely she didn't feel cold like she had done near other Virans.

Suddenly she heard the excited voice of someone running into the courtyard and calling out to the scholar. The scholar's fingers relaxed and slid away. The lid of the chest dropped heavily. She was safe – for now!

Chapter 6

The horseman had ridden day and night across the vast desert from the distant plains of India. Beneath his robes, he carried a sheaf of papers written in Sanskrit. On his journey, they had almost been stolen from him. The horseman could not read the papers, but he knew how important they were – how they had to reach the House of Wisdom without fail.

It was this horseman who had finally seen the jewel-like city of Baghdad in the distance. It was he who had ridden quickly through its busy streets. It was he who had demanded that the gates of the House of Wisdom be unlocked for him, and he who had run through the courtyards calling for the scholar. Finally it was he who had found the scholar at the moment he was about to open the chest where Neena hid.

Chapter 7

The scholar gripped the papers tightly. He sat heavily on the chest. Neena flinched as the lid groaned under his weight.

"So it is true," he said, staring into the eyes of the dusty horseman. "They have invented a new number."

The horseman shook his head. "I cannot imagine such a thing."

The scholar lowered his voice. "Come! We cannot discuss this here," he said. "It is too dangerous. A new number! It will change the way we think. It will change history."

A download from Tyler lit up Neena's Link: "Virans must be closing in," it said. "The papers have faded to almost nothing."

Neena knew she had to act. She climbed out of the chest and followed.

The two men entered the great library. The scholar paused by the guards at the doors. He did not want them to hear.

"You can go home," he told them.

Neena was sure that once inside, he was going to destroy the papers.

When the guards had gone, Neena crept into the huge room. It was stacked with papers, books and scrolls. The only place to hide was behind a large Persian rug hanging from a gallery. Quietly she climbed the gallery steps, squatted down, and waited for her moment.

"Nothing!" the scholar muttered. "The Indians call it 'sunya'. It means 'empty'. Zero."

"Zero!" Neena gasped. The number they had discovered was zero, a nought!

"But how can nothing be a number?" the horseman asked. "How can I count nothing? How can I measure a shape that has sides of nothing? There must always be *something*."

The scholar held the paper close to the flame of a lamp and stared hard. Neena tensed. Was he about to set fire to it?

"See!" he cried. He pointed at the figure '0' on the paper. "By using this number '0' we can write about one-ten, one-hundred, one-thousand, so easily. We could write any number using a combination of ten simple symbols – 0,1,2,3,4,5,6,7,8,9. Who knows what else it can do!"

"No one will ever know," a chilling voice hissed in the darkness. "Give."

"Who's there?" shouted the two men.

Chapter 8

Neena felt dizzy with fear. Where had the voice come from? There was nothing there.

A movement from the stone floor caught her eye. A metal grating, that led to the water channels beneath the city, slowly rose. Long ice-white fingers pushed the grating aside.

The Viran oozed from the hole like the darkest slime.

"Mine!" the Viran snarled, snatching the paper from the terrified men. Then he turned and jumped down the hole.

Without thinking, Neena grabbed hold of the Persian rug and slid down. The rug fell quickly after her, covering the two men in its folds.

The Viran was already wading along the
underground tunnel by the time Neena had
climbed into it. She could see his outline
some way ahead. Was he too far to catch? At
that moment her Link went off.

A download: "The paper is blank," it said
simply. Neena stopped. This couldn't be the
end of numbers, could it?

Neena began to run through the shallow water. She had to get close enough to the Viran for the Zaptrap to work.

Then the Viran stopped and turned. To Neena's horror, he began to run back towards her. With him, he brought an icy blackness like a chilling, dense stain along the tunnel.

From out of this cold darkness, the Viran's voice hissed. "You will never succeed."

Neena gripped her Zaptrap and pulled her arm back. As she threw it, she briefly wondered if it was safe near water.

The Zaptrap corkscrewed its way down the tunnel.

"Your number's up!" Neena screamed.

The Viran raised his arm and opened his mouth as if to shout, before exploding in a crackling shower of sparks.

There was no one in the library when Neena climbed back out of the tunnel. "They must have gone to get the guards," she thought.

As she placed the damp paper on the scholar's table, a download came from Tyler: "Ace! All writing back safely. Use position-finder on your Link. Location is 30 20 00 N. 44 26 05 E. Portal will be waiting to bring you home."

"Numbers!" she thought. "Where would we be without them?"

Tyler's Mission Report

Location:	Date:
Baghdad	Late 8th Century AD
Mission Status:	Viran Status:
Successful.	1 Viran zapped.

Notes: Solo mission by Neena. We think no one in Baghdad saw her.

I reckon that whenever people first came up with the idea of numbers, it was so they could count things – animals, stuff they owned, how many days. "One" and "Many" would no longer be enough.

But how often do you ever count zero animals or zero days? To count nothing is not counting – or is it?

Given that most counting started using fingers – groups of five and ten – the idea of zero never really came up. I mean, you'd never really think about 'no fingers'!

Count up to ten in your head. Did you start at zero? No. Now count down from ten. Zero appears! See! Zero is a number.

Sign off: ....Tyler...................

History: downloaded!
A Golden Age

The idea of zero was very nearly lost. Without zero, many ideas would not have developed in the way they have. We could have been living in a very different world. We wouldn't have computers, for a start!

Today, we have zero largely thanks to what happened in Baghdad in the 8th Century AD. At this time, a great thirst for knowledge and discovery grew throughout the Middle East. It was a golden age.

A school building in Baghdad

As part of this thirst for knowledge, travellers from the Middle East collected documents, books and manuscripts from all over the world.

Imagine it! From every direction, ideas came flooding in. Ideas that could be preserved, examined, developed. Imagine scholars searching through mountains of papers, translating the words they found written, hoping to discover a new idea.

Scholars in the House of Wisdom

It was not just books that came to Baghdad. People from many cultures travelled to this lively, energetic city. It is no wonder that some amazing discoveries were made, many of which are still with us today.

For more information, see the Time Chronicles website:
www.oxfordprimary.co.uk/timechronicles

Glossary

Baghdad *(page 11)* City built around 762 AD, on land between two great rivers, the Tigris and the Euphrates. Today it is the capital of Iraq. *"The newly-built city of Baghdad."*

gallery *(page 28)* A balcony or platform inside a building. *... a large Persian rug hanging from a gallery ...*

grating *(page 12)* A metal covering over the mouth of a tunnel or passageway. *... a dark figure pulled aside a grating and stepped into the underground water channel ...*

Persian rug *(page 28)* Hand-woven carpet from Persia (Iran).

Sanskrit *(page 6)* Ancient language from India, believed to be over 4000 years old. *"I think this one is written in Sanskrit ... "*

scholar *(page 17)* Somebody who spends their life studying. *The House of Wisdom – huge library run by world's leading scholars.*

scrolls *(page 16)* A roll of paper with writing (and sometimes pictures). *They were full of books and scrolls.*

water channel *(page 12)* A tunnel or an artificial river to take water to wherever it is needed.

Thesaurus: Another word for ...

flinched *(page 26)* recoiled, drew back.